How to Become a Famous Singer

*An Essential Guide
to Creating a Successful
Career as a Professional
Singer*

by Austin Landry

Table of Contents

Introduction

You've heard it over and over again:

"OMG! What a beautiful voice you have!"

"Have you thought about entering that singing contest?"

"Look out world, we've got the next Whitney Houston over here."

You know you can sing, but you haven't really thought about a singing career up until now, or at least you haven't taken the prospect seriously. Plus, a singing career seems really farfetched. In passing, you may have seen or read interviews of people in the music business giving testimonials of how hard it is to make it big in the industry. Then you look at your secure 9-to-5 job and brush aside the faintest idea of dropping it all to attempt a singing career. Nonetheless, you still really like to sing as a hobby, and people ask you to sing at their events and special occasions all the time. Remember that time you sang at your cousin's wedding? Or the numerous times you solo'd your heart out in your church? People in your community truly love to hear your voice. But unfortunately, to the rest of the world, you remain undiscovered or essentially nonexistent.

Then there are those of you who are seriously considering entering the music business, because you know you have the knack and talent for it. Not only are you talented, but you also like — no, *love* – getting up on stage, microphone in hand. If the chances of making it big weren't so slim, you'd be **all in**. Unfortunately, although it seems like a lucrative business for those who succeed, it also appears like a complete crap shoot as far as who becomes a superstar versus who remains singing for pennies at the local watering hole. Still, you have hope that someday, somehow you'll become one of the lucky few.

In either case – whether you're a skeptic, or a hopeful – there's one question you should ask yourself: Why **not** develop a money-making career doing something that you love? Do you really want to look back later and life, and think *"What if…"*?

This book is designed to help you bridge the gap between being the amateur singer you are now, and one who's using their voice to make a living (or even a killing). You'll learn how the internet has opened up new opportunities to aspiring singers like you, and you'll also be guided on everything from making your own original material to networking and marketing yourself, and signing up with labels.

Sure, singing at your cousin's wedding and getting thunderous rounds of applause is satisfying; but isn't it time for your passion to meet your purse? It's time to start dreaming bigger! There are so many new ways of making it big in the music biz, and the pages of this book are full of the tools you need to help make your dreams of becoming the next big thing a reality.

Chapter 1: Writing Original Music to Get Things Rolling

Original music is the core of every single artist's rise to fame. However, it is not everything. You can still be a successful and famous singer without having to sing an original song. This is especially true today in the age of internet services such as YouTube, SoundCloud, and other platforms in which new artists can show off their skills. If you search for your favorite song, and put the word 'cover' after, you will see a ton of videos with different people uploading their versions of these songs, and some of them have very decent views, some totaling in the millions.

Say what you want about Justin Bieber, but his career kicked off because he was uploading covers of famous songs on YouTube. There is also the option of television competitions that feature contestants who want to be the next big thing. Nearly 15 years ago, singing contests took off when Pop Idol launched in the UK. A year later, the format was adopted in the USA and American Idol was born. From then on, plenty of programs sprung up such as X Factor USA, The Voice, America's Got Talent, The Sing-Off, and so on. Singing competitions give you a more direct way into the entertainment industry, but don't expect an easy ride. We'll talk about this in more detail in the next two chapters.

The old and conservative way of making it big is to start off by writing your own songs. In the 80s and 90s, it was quite easy to record these songs using a simple tape recorder. In the digital age, it is even easier to record yourself. Plus, there are tools, some of them free of cost, which you could use to make your songs into something that can be listened to. If you are not a songwriter, you can learn how to do so. The process takes a bit of practice, but there is a little songwriter in everyone. Writing songs that people will like is another story. Here's how you can be a top songwriter of your own.

The first step in playing an instrument is optional, but many of the biggest artists know how to play at least one instrument. Knowing how to play an instrument helps you develop a better musical ear, and hence more melodies will come to you in your moments of inspiration. When you know how to play an instrument, you will learn many songs that don't have vocals in them, which will give you even more options of inspiration as you can draw melodies from them. First of all, you have to pick the instrument that best suits you. The two most popular instruments for songwriters are the piano and the guitar. These two instruments are easy to learn, and are also the most versatile. There are millions of songs that you can write for each of these instruments, and millions more that will be written for piano and guitar in the future.

Once you have chosen the instrument that suits you, it is time to start practicing. There are plenty of self-help books online that will help you learn an instrument without you having to hire a private teacher or go to a music school. Plus, there are additional online resources you can find on YouTube and other websites. On your journey, you will learn about arpeggios and scales. As a budding professional singer, arpeggios and scales will not be unfamiliar to you. You know that scales and arpeggios help in bettering your musical ear, and it can only improve further once you learn and practice doing them on your instrument. Once you've learned the basics of the instrument and you are comfortable enough with it to the point of playing basic chords along with your melody, it is time to start writing.

Writing music is an art, and there are very few people who are good enough to consistently write and perform hit music at the same time. The biggest pop icons write some of their songs, but a lot of their biggest hits are often written by other people. Only a few artists in the history of modern music could consistently write and perform hit music, such as the mega star Michael Jackson. This just goes to show how hard songwriting really is. You can like your own songs, but that doesn't mean other people will like them. Knowing what people will like comes thru experience and you will have to write a lot of songs until you get the right formula. Keep in mind the popular proverb "you have to crawl before you walk, and walk before you run."

Take the first steps by writing very simple songs with very simple chord progressions, and play them for your family and friends. Gauge their expressions, and tweak your songs to the way they reacted to your song. Also, it is important to study your audience, so if you play a modern song that only 15-30 year olds can appreciate, you will get a lot of negative responses. Once you do this several times, you can build up on your songs, by adding a bridge here, or adding some complex cords there. At this time, you are evolving past your family and friends, and you will have to play in front of acquaintances, schoolmates, and even total strangers. Use the same formula of gauging your audience's reactions, and work from there. You will be making hit music in no time.

Chapter 2:   Enter Singing Competitions

Singing competitions are nothing new, and they've been around for hundreds of years. Usually the winners of these competitions would win cash or kind, or recognition of some sort. But it wasn't until recently that singing competitions became big enough to launch a singing career instantaneously. We're talking about TV competitions, competitions that took off with the birth of Pop Idol in Britain about 15 years ago. It was so popular in the UK that it got adapted in the United States as the even more popular American Idol. X Factor was created and produced by Simon Cowell, the judge everyone loved to hate on American Idol. From the basic format, even more television contests sprouted up around the world. The careers of many popular artists took off, such as Kelly Clarkson, Ruben Studdard, Jennifer Hudson, Adam Lambert, Carrie Underwood, Jordin Sparks among others.

Singing contests have multiplied since American Idol's success, and it is now obvious how much of a lucrative business singing contests really are. We now have—15 years later—The Voice, X Factor USA, Rising Star, The Sing-Off, America's Got Talent, etc., and that's just in the USA alone. These television shows have been adapted in one form or the other in countries around the world. Signs are beginning to show that the world is getting a bit fatigued from these singing contests, but the money is still there, and the opportunities are still there.

Entering a competition is not an easy task, especially the television ones when there is a lot at stake. If you watch the backstory of the contestants of any singing competition on TV, 9 times out of 10 they will talk about singing for strangers and also singing at karaoke contests and the like. This is where a lot of successful professional singers start out, and this is where you might have to start out as well. You will not get to showcase your songwriting talents at a karaoke bar, but you will be able to show off your vocal skills, which is the most important part of becoming a famous singer. To be honest, most people don't really care that you can write music, all they care about is how you deliver your craft. Music is all about the emotions, and the analytical side of your brain is subdued in order for you to 'feel' the music you are listening to.

The purpose of entering small-time competitions, whether at your local bar, or your school, or your community, is not just to win a monetary prize, but to get experience for the bigger challenges ahead. If you are a stand-out singer, your competition will not be as strong as what you will experience in the final rounds of The Voice. The mega competitions brings the crème de la crème from different parts of the country, people equal to or even greater than you. So take these small competitions seriously, as you can't reach the top rung of the ladder without stepping on the first rung to begin with. If you are in a college or university, find out when a sorority/fraternity or club is hosting the next karaoke or open mic night, and enter. It doesn't even have to really be a contest, just enter. Ensure that you pick a song that will work up the crowd and entertain them. Picking the right song is essential, because if you go singing Ave Maria to a crowd that just got fed pop and hip hop songs, then you will be a pariah and maybe even a laughing stock. Yes people can appreciate Ave Maria, but there is a time and place for everything.

When you are about to enter that stage for the first time, it is important to psych yourself up for the performance ahead. Giving a good performance means that you will have to go up there with confidence, so singing Single Ladies while standing stiff as a board will make you come off as awkward. They won't be talking about your runs and vocals the next day, actually, they may not even be talking about you at all. If you can't dance, still show your awkward moves. What people want to see is you having fun while sounding pleasing to the ear at the same time. Your audience will respond positively to this, and you will have the crowd going wild. Of course it will be funny to some, but if your vocals are on point, nobody will realize how bad you are at dancing.

Once you have given the performance of a lifetime at your local talent show, it is time to step it up to an even bigger event. In almost every town you will find sing-offs and other singing competitions being held with a monetary reward for the winner. Depending on the town you are in, these competitions can be very rare, rare, slightly common, or very common. You have to constantly be on the look-out for any flyers advertising these events. You may even have to travel to another town for events like this, and in this case, Facebook and other social media sites will come in handy to learn of your next opportunity. Once you have entered the competition, the preparation begins. You will have to prepare for the competition the same way a professional artist prepares for a concert.

The first thing you should do is study your audience and the area that you will be performing in. Knowing the size and type of audience will then help you choose the correct songs to perform on the night. As we have said before, choosing the wrong song can be a very fatal choice in terms of your career. Unless it's a karaoke competition, ensure that the original song that you go with is tailor-made for your audience. Do constant breathing exercises and scales, because depending on the song you are performing, you will need your lungs to be at full capacity and your nerves to be as calm as possible. Once you have aced this part of your journey, you are ready for the big leagues. These competitions include regional and television competitions.

The guidelines for entering these competitions are a bit more strict and daunting. You will need proof that you are a good singer, so most likely you will need to send in an audition tape displaying your talents. The next process is auditions, where you perform in front of a small panel of judges to see if you are talented enough to be on the show. American Idol for instance, requires that participants do a song lasting no more than a minute in front of their judges a cappella. If they think you are good enough, then they will give you the green light to officially enter the competition. From here, you are set to start doing amazing things.

This part of the journey will be very tough, and takes a lot of guts. Not many people can survive these competitions, but you can take heart in the fact that many people who haven't won the competition go on to start successful careers. The aim is not to win, but to put yourself on the map. Of course, you will have to go in with a winning mentality in order to put your name on the map.

As we've said before, this is not for everyone. Not everybody will want to sing karaoke in front of millions of people for a shot at a record deal, and not many people will like the instant spotlight that will be on them. If entering the big time competitions is not for you, then you can show the world your talent through other means.

Chapter 3: Showcasing Your Music on YouTube

You are now writing your own music, and you are ready to showcase your talents to the world. Your music has been appreciated by your peers, your family and friends, and now you want to see if the world will like them too. The Internet Age started in the mid-2000s, and services which are widely used today were born, such as YouTube, Facebook and Twitter. Getting closer to the 2010s, other media services started to pop up that helped musicians get their music out there, such as Spotify, the rebranded Myspace, ReverbNation, SoundCloud, among others.

Let's not forget the behemoth that is iTunes though, the monster that sparked the digital music revolution 15 years ago. At the time, piracy was on the rise due to the increase in popularity of the .mp3 format and the ease of sharing these files. Plus there were services such as Napster which while 'legitimate', still made a lot of big wigs in the music industry unhappy. Almost out of the blue, Apple came out with the iPod, and iTunes, where people could buy music and put it on their iPods. From here, CD and album sales started to decline, but the sales of digital singles sharply rose. If you want to be taken seriously as a musician, then you will have to produce a single and place it on both iTunes and YouTube.

As a musician, don't expect to make much money from sales. Don't expect to sell a million records overnight. There are many musicians out there that are eating from Ramen cups daily, and that is the hard truth that you may have to face. In the following chapters, you will learn how you can market yourself to make people more aware of your craft, and bring in more money in the process. For now, focus on getting as many people as possible to listen to your music online, and the best way to do this independently is through YouTube.

YouTube has grown into the number one resource for music. Every day over a billion people visit YouTube, and a good chunk of those users just go there for the music. Music videos are the most popular videos on YouTube, and as a matter of fact, the top 10 most popular videos are all music videos. The most popular video of all is Psy's Gangnam Style, with over 2 billion views! However, since every YouTube video is free to listen to, YouTubers have to depend on people clicking on the ads on their videos. The less people clicking on those ads, the less money the YouTuber makes.

As a small indie artist, your options are not limited at all. They are actually pretty numerous. YouTube is not the only channel that you can upload your music to. As stated before, there is iTunes. However, people are moving away from the old model of buying music.

People are more interested in streaming these days, which is why YouTube is so popular, along with music-streaming platforms such as Spotify and Pandora.

Getting your music on Spotify and Pandora is a bit different though, because these services need to protect against copyright infringement, even more than YouTube. To get your music on these services, you will have to use an artist aggregator. These services handle the licensing and distribution of your music, kind of like what music labels do. Spotify and other music streaming services have a specific list of artist aggregators that they work with. You can visit their websites and look in the FAQ sections to see the services that they work with, so you can get your music on these platforms.

The most important thing about getting your music out there is to make sure that your music doesn't suck, and that the quality is top-notch. If you upload terrible music, then you will get terrible returns. This is why it is important that you take the steps that have been outlined before this chapter, because just like starting any new business, you will have to test your market first, to ensure that you get a perfect fit. If you don't have a perfect fit, then you will be singing the wrong things to the wrong people, and you will inevitably fail. Make sure that your songs are properly produced, and if you are a newbie at producing—

where you have been doing it for under 2 years—then it's best that you hand the producing reins over to a veteran. It will cost you, but having music online that not only doesn't sell but also creates a bad reputation for you, will cost you even more.

Now that you have your music online, it is time to market your music. Spotify and the like will not market your music for you, until they are sure that your music will bring more plays and more money to them. This section is very hard, even with social media. Do not fall into the trap of believing that social media is simple and easy, because it is not. We are here to prevent you from making the same mistakes a lot of indie artists make.

Chapter 4: Marketing Yourself on the Internet

Your music is now on YouTube, iTunes and Spotify. However, no one is viewing, downloading or listening to your music. Many new artists get frustrated at this stage, and give up. Some still stick with the old mindset of marketing their music through radio, and think that the radio is still a powerful marketing tool. Your most popular marketing tool is the internet, and social media sites are your main agents. Over 2 billion people visit social media sites around the world, on their computers and on their cellphones. Some media sites and apps allow you to reach the full audience of the site instead of just your network. Facebook is a site that helps you interact with a closely knit network. Those networks are often small and filled with family and friends who are already familiar with your music. If you really want to reach a global audience, then making a Facebook page is the key.

Facebook pages are much harder to maintain than a regular user account, as you will have to find ways to reach tens, hundreds, thousands and even millions of networks on the site. Facebook gives tools to help marketers and page owners reach the people that they want, but often this kind of work will have to be given to the pros. Facebook's algorithms prevent information overload and noise in people's News Feeds by filtering out posts it thinks that a user doesn't want to see. Your job as a page owner is to get Facebook to bring your page to as many people as possible. There are many ways to do this, which includes buying ads, promoted stories and sharing memes.

The buying of ads is probably the safest and most reliable way to get to the audience that you want, but it is also the most expensive. With ads and promoted stories, you can target the people you want to see a specific post, or direct people to looking at and liking your page. When someone likes your page, then Facebook will put more content from your page onto their News Feeds. However, Facebook's pesky algorithms will step in again eventually if the person who liked your page isn't looking at your posts anymore, so your posts will begin to get filtered out. To remain in your fans' News Feeds, you will have to post often, It doesn't have to be just about your music, and as a matter of fact, it shouldn't be just about your music. This is where the sharing of memes comes in, something you don't have to do, but what a lot of pages seem to be resorting to these days.

A meme is a popular idea that is shared and built-on in some way or another as it is being shared. Popular memes on Facebook are those pictures with captions beneath them. These pictures depict a certain idea, and when they are shared, the idea is either being built upon or being changed. Some memes die quickly, while others live on for a very, very long time. If you can't afford ads, then you will have to make people think, feel and/or laugh. Memes get high click-rates, and if you play your cards right, people will see your page connected to that meme and will want to like your page. Then the process of acquiring and keeping users starts again. It can be very exhausting, but very rewarding at the same time. You won't get money directly through Facebook, unless you open a store, but you will get a following and a fanbase which will start listening to your music. So, if you go the meme route, ensure that your page produces enough solid content to show your fanbase who and what you really are. There are widgets which you can install in your Facebook page that allow your fans to listen to your music for free. If you have plenty of YouTube videos, ensure that you share the links of those videos on your Facebook page, and the number of views your videos get will increase. If people like your music enough, they will share it and bring even more views and listens to your music. You can also use Facebook Video as well, which seems to be the default choice for video uploads for Facebook pages these days.

Facebook is not the be-all end-all, however. There are plenty of ways to market your music to the billions of people online without having stepped foot into Facebook's walled garden. There is the global network of Twitter, a service which is known to get content to worldwide audiences very quickly. On Twitter, one makes tweets, which can be shared by retweeting. The more people that retweet, the more people that see your tweet. This is a better way of getting your content out there quickly than you could with Facebook, but it is worse than Facebook in the way your post can get buried in the noise.

Twitter and Facebook are just a minority. Other apps and services you should try out are Tumblr, Snapchat and Instagram. Just remember these services are all free, so there's no excuse for not having an account on at least one of them. You can learn to do social media marketing yourself, even though it is not easy. You don't even need social media, as you could buy ads online where they can be put on an endless number of websites, and you could also have plugins on your website which play snippets of your music. Marketing online is a very stressful job though. Hiring a PR firm or agent will get your music out there with less hassle, but with a heftier cost.

Chapter 5: Networking and Signing up with Labels

If you are going the indie route, then this may not be for you. You don't have to sign with a label to be successful. The services that labels provide can be received elsewhere, but they may be harder to come by and in some cases less reliable. Also, people like to see that an artist is attached to a specific label. They perceive an artist not attached to a specific label as a *nobody*. It's a sad state of affairs in today's world, but fortunately, that outdated point of view is dying fast with the rise of streaming services like Spotify. Spotify has numerous areas on their platform in which people can listen to indie music, which makes it an excellent platform for indie musicians, along with YouTube and SoundCloud. But for the majority of you who don't want to take the risk of the indie route, then signing with a label is the best thing to do.

Before thinking of signing-up with a label, there are certain things to keep in mind. Don't expect labels to be your buddies. They don't care about you, all they care about is the amount of money that you can bring them. If you are not bringing them any money, then they will cut you from their label without hesitation. All labels care about is their profits, so ensure that you are producing top-quality music first before you even utter anything about labels.

Getting noticed by execs at a certain label follows the same procedure as getting people to follow your brand on social media. You have to market yourself properly in order to catch the eyes and ears of the people you need to capture the attention of. It also involves you signing at many different events, as much as you can, and taking your talent on the road.

Most times, the record label won't come to you, but you will have to go to the record label to get a deal. Finding the record label that is right for you and that will accept you is as hard as applying for Ivy League schools. Just like auditioning for a talent show, send in your best performance demo, and let the label you are courting get to know the real you and get to listen to your best music. Remember, the music that you send them has to be produced at the highest quality, so hire a producer if you need to.

Finally, if you hate the networking process, then you can hire your own manager. These people are good at meeting new people and making new connections, so they will help you get better deals with better labels, and also get your name out there.

Conclusion

The life enjoyed by famous artists like Lady Gaga, Beyoncé, Adam Levine, Justin Timberlake and others didn't come overnight. They had to start very small, sing at small events, sign up with small labels, until they could sing at larger events and sign up with larger labels. They had to network to get their names out there, and it took years for people to buy their albums and singles.

In the more modern society, the era of YouTube, SoundCloud and Spotify, artists have found easier ways to market themselves without having to hire PR firms and personnel. However, with the increase of new opportunities, came the increase in competition and noise.

Some believe it is much harder for quality new artists to become famous today than in the past. Don't be dismayed by the noise. You just have to find ways to rise above the noise, and there are plenty of ways to do just that. Once you follow the steps we have outlined in this book, you will be on your way to stardom.

Finally, I'd like to thank you for purchasing this book! If you enjoyed it or found it helpful, I'd greatly appreciate it if you'd take a moment to leave a review on Amazon. Thank you!

Printed in Poland
by Amazon Fulfillment
Poland Sp. z o.o., Wrocław